The Kingdom

A Children's Story of Identity and Inheritance

JerriAnn Webb

WestBow Press books may be ordered through booksellers or by contacting:

WestBow Press
A Division of Thomas Nelson & Zondervan
1663 Liberty Drive
Bloomington, IN 47403
www.westbowpress.com
1 (866) 928-1240

ISBN: 978-1-9736-3167-5 (sc)
ISBN: 978-1-9736-3168-2 (e)

Library of Congress Control Number: 2018907310

Print information available on the last page.

WestBow Press rev. date: 6/22/2018

WESTBOW
P R E S S®
A DIVISION OF THOMAS NELSON
& ZONDERVAN

There once was a Kingdom.
And it began with a King...
A magnificent, imaginative,
wonderous King!

A King who is love,
who never could lie.
A King who is good.
A King who is wise.

A brilliant, Love King,
full of delight!
Full of laughter and giggles
and rapturous Light!

And The King spoke into darkness
"Let there be light!" [1]
He spoke and divided
the day from the night.

And glorious King Creator,
then spoke into time
joyously creating
a Garden, of incomparable design.

[1]   Genesis 1:3 "And God said, Let there be light, and there was light." NLT (New Living
Translation)

He spoke such resplendence
As the grasses, they grew!
They sang of His radiance;
trees with seed bearing fruit.

And He looked at the oaks
and dolphins and sun.
He looked with great pleasure
at all He had done.

Dinosaurs and redwoods
stretching to sky!
Waterfalls cascading
and bright butterflies!

Patterns and hues,
the greenest of greens!
Breathtaking landscapes,
unparalleled scenes!

Jaw-dropping splendor
and exquisite displays
of a loving Creator
unsurpassed in His ways.

And in the Garden, a people.
A most precious creation.
The Creator now Father
birthing a nation.

He made them like Him!
Adam then Eve.
He put breath in their lungs
to live and be free!

The King placed them in charge.
There they belonged!
Destined to rule
the Garden, their home.

And so, in the people,
an assignment bestowed
from a Father so faithful
from whom all goodness flowed.

Completion. Perfection.
The Father's design.
The language of Heaven
to be yours! To be mine!

And perhaps you know the story,
you may know it too well,
of a serpent accuser
with deception to sell.

Thoughts creeping and seeping,
into Eve's mind.
You can be like God...
...who you are is a lie.

And with a turn of events,
catastrophic infection
entered the Kingdom
through rebellious rejection.

In a deceptive and tempting,
tantalizing, bad trick
the deceiver deceived
and made the world sick.

And Adam and Eve
with regret and sad shame
lost the key to the Kingdom
and gave their domain

to a serpent, now Foe,
pride twisted, unfurled,
as the weight of the sadness
ripped through the world.

And then heartache ensued,
unimaginable pain
seen in every generation
and in each family name.

Oh, but The King!
The King of pursuit!
He would never stop loving
and looking for you!

He would go to great lengths
to restore what was lost.
He would search for His beloved
at passionate cost!

In the greatest love story
to right what was wrong,
The King pursued His sons and daughters
to bring them back home.

And Light broke through silence
as King Father sent Son!
To redeem what was lost.
To undo what was done.

In a move unsurpassed
the Last Adam He came!
A Man had to get back
what a man gave away.

And there in the manger
a Savior's heartbeat!
And there on the cross
our freedom complete!

And out of the tomb
dominion then won!
A commission to reign
as daughters and sons!

The King resurrected a Kingdom
in you and in me!
Jesus now Lord
of a people redeemed!

Rest and shalom.
Connection again.
Our identity found
only in Him.

A new Kingdom nature!
Royal and true!
Holy Spirit given
to empower you!

Immeasurable inheritance!
A gift from the King!
Within you God's Spirit
can live and can sing!

And now...

There is a Kingdom.
It is fully restored,
and you are the Heir
of exponentially more

than you could ever imagine
cause the Kingdom is near!
We can all live like Jesus
'cause the Kingdom is here!

And the King calls you friend!
You are lovely and kind!
You are righteous in Christ!
And you have the King's mind!

You are solution
to a world who needs you!
You carry His power.
You know what to do!

You have authority.
You now have the key.
Son and daughter, today,
see what He sees!

Speak and speak up
as your future unfolds!
Be brave and courageous!
There are feats to be told

of all The King will do
through you, through your life!
He has positioned you now
at this moment in time...

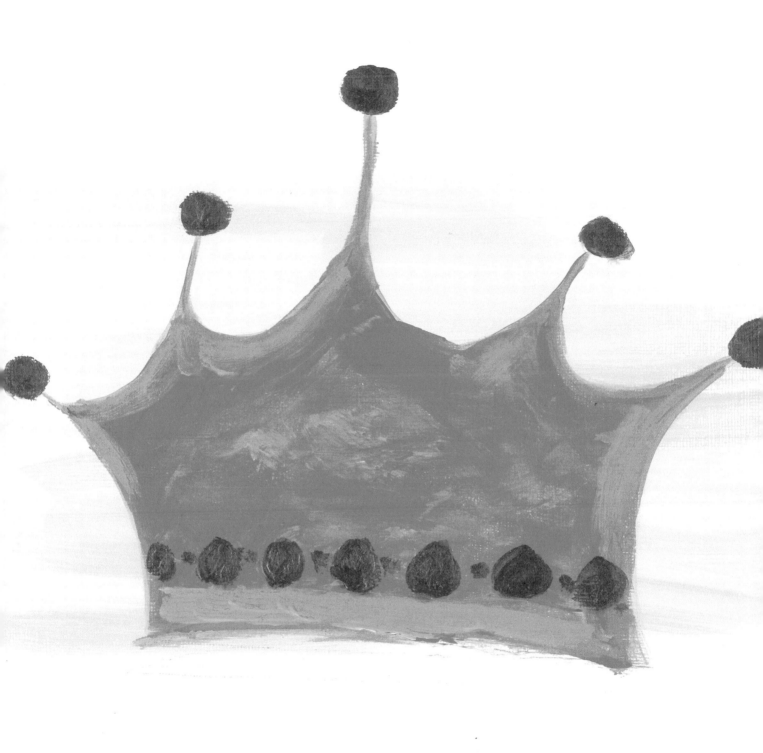

to know who you are in the Kingdom.
The world is waiting for you.

Glossary

1. Identity - The first thing God gave us! We are made in God's image to resemble and represent Him. We are made in God's likeness to function and operate like Him. See Genesis 1:26-28.

2. Inheritance – Gifts, promises, resources, and access to whatever you need from The King! Jesus died on the cross to forgive us of sin. How amazing! He also died and was resurrected so we could live a free and powerful life now! He has given us so many gifts, like the Holy Spirit. God wants you to know He has promises for you! He wants you to know what resources are available to you now as The King's kid!

3. Assignment – God told us who we are, and then He gave us something to do (assignment). We have work to do! We can all live like Jesus! We can showcase God's goodness in all we do and say!

4. Deception – Believing a lie and not even knowing it is a lie.

5. Catastrophic – a word used to describe something horrible. When sin entered the Kingdom, it caused a disastrous separation between God and His kids.

6. Domain – your home!

7. The Last Adam – Jesus is the last Adam. Jesus came to restore the relationship Adam lost in the garden. Jesus came and restored the Kingdom! See 1 Corinthians 15:45.

8. Dominion – Authority

9. Commission – God has authorized us as His sons and daughters to display His glory!

10. Shalom – Wholeness. Because of Jesus, we can be whole and happy in every way!

11. Exponentially – Always increasing! God has new and wonderful gifts to give you every morning!

Printed in the United States
By Bookmasters